Portrait of the Artist as a White Pig

Portrait of the

Artist as a White Pig

JANE GENTRY

Poems

LOUISIANA STATE UNIVERSITY PRESS   BATON ROUGE

This publication is supported in part by an award from the
National Endowment for the Arts.

Published by Louisiana State University Press
Copyright © 2006 by Jane Gentry
All rights reserved
Manufactured in the United States of America
First printing

Designer: Melanie O'Quinn Samaha
Typeface: Minion Pro, Gotham
Typesetter: G & S Typesetters, Inc.
Printer and binder: Edwards Brothers, Inc.

Library of Congress Cataloging-in-Publication Data
Gentry, Jane.
  Portrait of the artist as a white pig : poems / Jane Gentry.
    p.   cm.
  ISBN-13: 978-0-8071-3169-5 (alk. paper)
  ISBN-10: 0-8071-3169-5 (alk. paper)
  ISBN-13: 978-0-8071-3170-1 (pbk. : alk. paper)
  ISBN-10: 0-8071-3170-9 (pbk. : alk. paper)
  I. Title.
PS3557.E462P67   2007

811'.54—dc22
                                                                          2005034824

The author offers grateful acknowledgment to the editors of the following publications, in which poems in this book originally appeared, sometimes in slightly different form: *Hollins Critic,* "Portrait of the Artist as a White Pig" (February 2004); *Limestone,* "Desire" (2000); *Louisville Review,* "A Human House," "Sleeping with You" (both Spring 2002); *Sewanee Review,* "Hunting for a Christmas Tree after Dark," "Roofer" (both Summer 2002), "The Concept of Morning" (forthcoming), "Penelope's Night Out" (forthcoming); *Taint* (online magazine), "By Your Small Lake" (Winter 2004); *Heartland Review,* "Diana, of a Certain Age, Takes a Bath" (Spring 2005); *Coffee Talk Quarterly,* "Sam's Club in Winter" (Winter 2005), "Realty" (Summer 2005). "The Song of the Furnace" appeared in *Writing Who We Are: Poems by Kentucky Feminists,* ed. Elizabeth Oakes and Jane Olmsted (Bowling Green: Western Kentucky University, 1998). "The Red Taffeta Dress" and "Hunting for a Christmas Tree after Dark" appeared in *A Kentucky Christmas,* ed. George Ella Lyon (Lexington: University Press of Kentucky, 2003). "Portrait of the Artist as a White Pig" also appeared as a broadside (Adela Press, 1996) and in the chapbook *A Year in Kentucky: A Garland of Poems* (Press Eight Seventeen, 2005). "April in Your Garden," "Waking Up, in May," "Nearby," "At Harmony Landing," "Diana, of a Certain Age, Takes a Bath," "Taking the Train from Maysville to New York," and "The Traveler" also appeared in the chapbook *A Year in Kentucky.*

The author wishes to thank the Kentucky Arts Council, the University of Kentucky, and the Art Group for their various gifts of attention, time, and money that supported her work on these poems.

The paper in this book meets the guidelines for permanence and durability of the Committee on Production Guidelines for Book Longevity of the Council on Library Resources. ∞

In memory of Bill
and for Lucy and Susannah

Life in this world is full of pain. But pain, which is the contrary of pleasure, is not necessarily the contrary of happiness or joy.
—Thomas Merton, *Seeds of Contemplation*

. . . he who kisses the joy as it flies
lives in eternity's sunrise.
—William Blake, *Several Questions Answered*

Contents

One

A Human House	3
The Concept of Morning	5
Roofer	6
Desire	8
From My Attic Window	9
Among the Stations of the Cross on the Grounds of Taylor Manor Nursing Home	10
Waking Up, in May	11
Riddle	12
The News	14
Diana, of a Certain Age, Takes a Bath	15
The Song of the Furnace	16
Realty	17
November	18
Sam's Club in Winter	19
Hunting for a Christmas Tree after Dark	20

Two

My Life Story	23
In the House with the Red Roof	24
The Red Taffeta Dress	25
Their Bed	26
My Mother's Rooms	27
Leaving the Shades Up	29
Ultrasound	30
Aubade	31
To My Grandson, in the Womb, on Washington Heights	32
Skating	34

Your Company	35
Sitting with Aunt Mary in Hospice	36
The Reading Lamp	37
Eating a Pear from the Tree My Father Planted Thirty-One Years Ago	38
One Summer in the Life of My Mother	40

Three

Portrait of the Artist as a White Pig	47
At Pleasant Hill, Kentucky, in January	48
Taking the Train from Maysville to New York	50
The Light at the End of the Tunnel	52
Utopia: An Idyll	53
Rose Week in the Brooklyn Botanic Garden	54
On the Eve of War with Iraq	56
My Two Daughters in Paris	57
Nike of Samothrace	58
Les Jardins du Luxembourg	60
Leaving the Sidewalk Café	61
Portrait of Sue Richards as a Young Girl	62
The Clouds, My Mother	63
Watching Stars	64
Parable of the Reverse Sunset	65
First Kiss	66
April in Your Garden	67
Nearby	68
By Your Small Lake	69
At Harmony Landing	70
Penelope's Night Out	71
Sleeping with You	72
The Traveler	73
The Chain: A True Account	74

One

A Human House

To have a task that takes you
below ground to the basement,
feeling your legs spring under
you as you descend the steps
to pull the shirts, dry, off
the clothesline by the furnace.
Then to fold them, and the towels,
and ascend through the rooms
of the house, with the perfume
of cleanliness rising
in your nose. To see sunlight
falling on the rug of the upstairs
hall, to feel the June air
move across the bedroom
as if you walked in the head
of a tree. To climb
to the attic closet carrying
winter clothes, wool scratching
your arms. To fling open
the windows to release
the stale air. Then to sit
in your chair on the porch,
reading maybe, or writing a letter
you've owed for months;
to watch the shifting sky
through the thinning branches
of the yellowwood tree.
All day to inhabit!
Like a fox in her den,
a bird in a knothole,
an ant in its tunnel,
I belong here. My house
is as real in the world
as water or air,
as the birds' clear vowels
that rise through fading
light at the day's end.

And then, after night falls,
to stand in the dark backyard
looking into the golden light
of the rooms you inhabit
in the house that is your
body's body, and to see
on the kitchen table
the voluptuous wine
in the dark mysterious bottle
which you at supper all but emptied.

The Concept of Morning

> But what interests me here is the specific mystery of sleep partaken of for itself alone, the inevitable plunge risked each night by the naked man, solitary and unarmed, into an ocean where everything changes, the colors, the densities, and even the rhythm of breathing, and where we meet the dead.
>
> —*Marguerite Yourcenar,* Memoirs of Hadrian

I arise from the grave of the bed.
I re-muscle from the lapse into nothingness.
I put the self back on like a shirt.
I re-affix my face. I crack the egg
of the closed eye.

I open my eyes to light, to its comforting
habits of color, of patterns in the rug,
in the flowers on the drapes, in the sunlit
veneer of my dresser, in the shifting
leaves outside my window. These shapes
enfold me like a second mother's arms.

I am retold out of the gibberish of the night,
composed again from the junk of dreams,
from the chaos of the blood drumming
in the veins like a river running
toward the night when we cease being:
practicing, practicing.

Roofer

I

He squats, sticky as a fly on the roof's
steep pitch. It's all in the angle
of his feet to his ankles, in the bend
of his knees. Loose-jointed as a dancer,
he sits tight, tilting his head
this way, then that to see the shingle
fitted straight. He doesn't touch
the cigarette that trues itself, dangling
from his lips.

I've come awake this January morning to the sound
of crowbars wrenching at my neighbor's garage,
to the crack of hammers, methodic, knowing.
Nothing frantic in these sounds as old as shelter,
as familiar. I see him stand, jointlessly unfolding,
pull from the holster on his hip the shingle knife,
as easy as you'd pluck the fork beside your plate.
From my second-story window, I see him walk
along the sky edge into the crooked arms
of the apple tree. On his khaki shorts
I see black patterns of his scooting.

At home among the highest branches, he stands,
bone relaxed, muscle lapsed, arms akimbo,
and talks to his partner on the ground.
I see their words, their laughs, but cannot
hear them. Into a green wheelbarrow, his cohort
loads the flung-off shingles, while,
at the zenith, the roofer, on his haunches now,
begins to cut, like feather into wing, each
outer shingle to its edge, its proper place.
At the lower corner, he balances one leg
out upon the air as comfortably
as if it rested on a hassock.

II

By the end of this short winter day, there
have been at least three weathers: a sudden
drenching shower; then windy, cutting sunshine;
and now dark cold closes in. The roofer hauls
his hand under the sparse lift of his hair.

The woman of the house, her arms around themselves,
steps out to chat him up about the job.
They pantomime. He smokes, hammers, too,
in the same deft rhythm, positions the nail.
With one stroke, it is home. He stands
again, two-handed, reaches in his apron pocket
languorously as if to scratch himself.
His foot slips at the corner as he talks
and smokes and turns to shift. No bother. Only
start the move again. He cuts and flings
the trimmed-off pieces in a careful heap beside
the woman. He stands, oblivious to wind
and coming dark, to look at what is done
and what remains to be done.

Desire

My cat in the sill,
hunched mean as a fist,
steely as a coiled spring,
studies a foolishness of sparrows
in the tree outside the window.
A pounce in check, she holds
her ears erect like wings of bats
that sail out upon the air
buoyant with what they hunger
to snap up, rend, pulverize,
swallow into the lustful
muscle of such flight.

From My Attic Window

I see the roofs of neighbors' houses,
and the muscle of a bird's back as it flies
into the red ribs of sunset
beyond the courthouse clock.

All that sideways light
gilds the familiar, singes
the dark spine of the yellowwood
in my backyard, my sway-backed garage,
the house next door,
and lays long black shadow out
behind them like an overleaf.

Across the field
that I can only see the edge of
shines my mother's window
(another face behind it now),
from which she watched
each night darkening the world.

Among the Stations of the Cross on the Grounds of Taylor Manor Nursing Home

After a long winter and a cold March comes the first warm day.
Under the mild sky a farmer in the next field calls his cattle.
"Ho-up," he sings out of his belly, and from under the bill of his cap.
Doves hoo their cries of love; robins' declarations fill the air.
The cows, rough in their winter fur, saunter sedately spaced
into sight. After them, the haunchy calves tumble through the gate,
then the wandery newborns. I stand among the Stations of the Cross,
amid the Sisters of St. Joseph buried in a circle. "Lord, help me
to bear the partings that must come," says the stone I stand beside.
I turn to face the nursing home and the flowery hill where
my demented mother once scourged every dandelion.
The wind's small breath implies sweet grassy dung.
A crow, still stubby-tailed, stands on one foot, then
the other, on the top branch of a tall, bare tree.

Waking Up, in May

The bass of the thunder
rises beyond the locusts,
under the hill. Closer,
another voice answers.
The knowing grackle
trills its three-notes,
moves here, there
among expectant leaves.
Then rain begins,
taps out rhythms,
rolls its slurred notes down
the roof. Thirsty grass
opens its mouths, and tight,
new gardens breathe, unfurl
beneath the drumming torrents.

The quick baton
of lightning!

In downspouts and gutters,
rapturous phrasings,
downpouring streams.

Riddle

Made of movement, but moving nothing
in order to move, I ride myself
through the grass. No warmth of my own,
I depend on the sun. Always as wary
as you are, I fear the cold wind,
the sun behind the clouds, and darkness
that lasts so long I must hole up
below-ground bound in circles
of myself and sleep the winter out. But now
June sun heats the garden path, and singes
the pillow of rock on which the sundial sits.
All morning, over the top of your book
you spy me flashing like a needle
along your vision's hem, stitching
light to shadow, sage to thyme.
Eye-quick, you see not me but zigzag
trembling of the yarrow, until I levitate
into the narrowness beneath the sundial.

By noon, my oven's fiery, and I,
near melting, pour out into the ivy
bordering the garden. Air shimmies
above the bricks, and I, disinhibited
by heat I've drunk so recklessly,
just drop myself in loops, heedless
of the gardener with his hoes
and other handles passing back
and forth about his work.

Then I'm gone—my notice sudden is.
It bothers you to lose my place.
Furtively, in golden light you rise,
fold your book, and as you walk inside
are stopped—a tighter breathing!
There am I risen, too,
toward the sun, on the closest log
of the woodpile, my spotted shaft

draped artfully in camouflage
among the pulp. My lidless eyes
proclaim me to you as I am, as what
you see but cannot know: the bright
black bead of zero in my gaze
unblinking at the dark, the cold.

What am I?

The News

Nothing is gladder than morning:
sunshine fallen like new pennies
through the backyard trees. All the sounds
of beginning: crows warring overhead,
children shouting on their way to school,
cars accelerating, carrying people to work.
The flame of impatiens out my kitchen window,
the cat, hungry, nipping my ankles,
the slap of my neighbor's screen door
as she turns her face to the sky,
then bends to pick up the news of this day.

Diana, of a Certain Age, Takes a Bath

My body is drifting out of its familiar shape
like a great, slow cloud in August.
My muscled calves deflate,
my cheekline sags,
my waist fattens.
After the chase
I still enjoy my bath, the luxury
of perfume on my breasts,
my neck, my thighs,
as Nofretete did, or Cleopatra,
just as in my salad days.

But sometimes in the mornings now,
fresh from sleep, I skin off
my gown before the mirror
and the girl I used to be,
my flawless pearly body,
suddenly appears to me,
rises tranquil as the moon
gliding out of clouds,
and strikes me breathless
as at the forest pool
when I spied Actaeon in his blind
(his arrows useless in his quiver),
drinking in new quarry:

the shining of my body,
fulsome and deadly as his hunter's eye.
Terrified as the deer I turned him into,
I, too, am dogged by what I know is coming.

The Song of the Furnace

In the mirror my lower face diminishes
when I smile, and a tissuey wrinkle deepens
under my eyes. I am almost old.
Am I brave enough to be alone?
In this moment, my furnace sings
all through the house its burden
of comfort. My body, bent to
the shape of a question mark,
warms on my bed covered in fall sun.
My mind somersaults in an ecstasy
of near-sleep. Excepting the comma
of my cat, fitted to the hollow
of my arc, there is no creature
I think I need inside this peace.
A voice might cut
like the hard side of a hand
against the long throat
of this song.

Realty

Rows of new homes, tidy in plastic siding, come
creeping over the hill toward the clapboard house
collapsing into its center under its own weight,
its porch barely clinging, that was built to fit exactly
the farmer's rocker, the wife's churn, her canning table.

This bulldozed valley, pocked with manholes,
will not be dark again for eons, its trees uprooted
that broke the winter wind and made the summer shade,
that stood beneath the fixed stars the farmer watched.

By the truckload, window assemblies and doors in frames
daily arrive in the raw streets, while the house, its angles
all askew, falls into its own pit, a mouth hungry
as its fireplace where the windy tongues inflamed
the black throats of all the chimney chinks.

November

brings its own odd comforts,
mercury dropping,
gray all over:
the highway where I'm driving,
the sky clamped shut against the earth,
the earth itself.
Even the trees dissolve
into their own gray smoke

and long ago gray dusks,
when I lay on the scratchy rug
listening to the radio
while my mother hummed, filling
the rooms with supper smells,
and, on the blackening windows,
my breaths made a blistery skin
I could not see through.

Sam's Club in Winter

Freezers long as freight cars chock full of rock-
hard cakes, pies, lasagnas, plastic sacks of crucifers
(when I unseal a door, its breath resists and sighs).

Rows of hot, baked hens, taut with succulence.
Chicken breasts cradled in styrofoam, corded like firewood.

A spill of fresh fruits from the tropics and the underside
of earth: beguiling little crates of clementines, nubile
grapes in see-through plastic. A grove of greenery
and banks of flowers, each blossom netted against bruising;
shelves tall as trees, toilet tissue stacked up into darkness.

Outside, winter's first Alberta clipper nudges around
the corners of the big box, pokes the thin skin of plenty.

Hunting for a Christmas Tree after Dark

A sudden mildness in the cold field.
Scraps of snow still strewn on the hillside.
The net of stars cast out overhead.
The shapes of old cedars come toward me
familiar as loved bodies approaching
from a long way off.
The creek in a hurry, as full of itself
as a zipper, the slow-melting snow.

I can hardly make out the rock fence
wavering up the hill, cold stone
on cold stone, stacked together
by unknown hands so many years ago.

How grateful I am for this moment of peace
my body has made with gravity, this
pulling things out of their places
and holding them in,
like Orion the hunter, who, when I blink,
seems to throw his leg over the low fence
of the horizon and climb into this bound with me.

Up ahead, looking for the one perfect tree,
my cousin John. His lantern bobs through
the dark meadow. He raises the globe
of light over and over in prospect.
I hang back, feeling rich in the black
waste, safe in this bowl of earth,
with rocks outcropping in the flattened grass,
trees wet, dirt sweetened by the downhill run-off
of all fear. Though the Interstate throbs
and the town lights bleed into the blot
of circling trees, from here the stars redeem
the dark that makes them shine.

Two

My Life Story

I stood in my crib. Dust floated in a shaft of light.
I splashed in a metal tub on a sunny porch.

The years took the mule barn, its mountains of hay,
its ladder to the loft, and columns of sun
where swam the sweet talcum of flyaway earth.

The years took my stringy body that scrabbled
up the ladder, that could bend in circles over
backwards, and turn itself in cartwheel
after cartwheel across the shady grass.

Eventually, the tall banks of August clouds
and fire tongues in the grate on winter nights
spoke to me of a new life,
promising richer days and nights to come.

The years took our house, cool and dark,
generous as a healthy heart, where in September
a cricket sang under the kitchen hearth.

They took my mother with her red hair
and her creamy skin, and my father
whose laughing head shone with the fire
of summer as he shoveled corn to his pigs.

When I awoke one day, my bloom
was past. Those who loved me first were dead,
and promises had blown away like chaff
or clouds, which dazzle now only in the moment
of their height and roll.
The years have given back the thing itself.

In the House with the Red Roof

I lie in my crib watching
dust drift through sunshine.
I see the pipe holding
the orange-hot stove
to the chimney bricks.
I see the shut white door
Mother clicked behind her
when she left
me. I hear a cricket
singing under the staircase
and the drone of an airplane
in the blue sky of the window.
Then I hear the ringing
of no sound at all, no sound
of her footsteps on the floor.

The Red Taffeta Dress

On Christmas Eve it was under the tree
in a long, flat box. My family's faces,
washed in colored light, turned on me.
I was afraid it was clothes.
But when I tore the tissue off
I loved the sight of it,
a dress as red as Sleeping Beauty's.

In Granny's cold bedroom, Mother pulled it
over my head. She'd sewn it right: it swept
the floor and framed my face to prettiness.
I walked out into the gazes of cousins,
aunts, uncles, grandparents, father.
How like a skin it was, wedding me
to the dream, a sure joining,
the red dress fitting my child body
like a lost piece in the puzzle of the world.

Their Bed

Tonight I go to sleep to thunder over the fields
and summer rainfall like my mother's voice
when she lay beside my father in their bed,
each of its posts heavy as a tree.
Rain dripped through trumpet vines
outside their open window.
I knew they pleased each other: he loved
her milky body, her hair like fire,
her fingers always doing. She loved
his wide laugh, his ease with cattle,
his biceps, hard as hedge balls,
that he squeezed in knots for us to feel.
In their bed they lay notched like forks
in the kitchen drawer. From my bed I heard
them talk about the rain—it brings on hay,
makes big tobacco leaves. Stiff with listening,
I hear what they heard (the fall of water,
heaving trees), and I drift away, carried
into the dark on swift currents of their comfort.

My Mother's Rooms

The rooms of Mother's house shone
with cleanliness and order. My father
lived there, too, but he and all
his habits, inside their house,
seemed also of my mother.
In her rooms, daylight was good
in every season. She read up
on architecture and situated
this last house on the hill's lap,
sheltered by the upward slope
and brightened by the falling
westward prospect in the front.
Then she planted trees: an ash
outside the kitchen window,
two hollies out the back, a stand
of pines along the fencerow,
with volunteer wild cherries up
and down. They grew tall,
but never close enough to darken.

The objects in her rooms gleamed
with careful choosing, and polish
from loved hands before her own.
The clock's voice, merry as a heartbeat,
circulated through the rooms.
Newly wed, my parents bought
the clock at auction at a death house
on Boone's Creek, where they also
got the coal hod that sat beneath
the mantel where the clock stood,
and a Currier and Ives in which a man
in a hat drew a bucket from a well.
Each piece, a bright stone set
just right, seemed to have grown
there in the green light, brighter
yet for her small resentment
of the weekly dusting.

These rooms were their backdrop
until their lives began to fray:
their cancers and dementia
quickened by a son broken
in a car wreck, a daughter
marrying contrary to her best,
one grandchild neglected,
another always sad—
they could not set things right.
Then came my father's sickbed,
skewed into the room
with the hod, the clock,
and the picture of the young man
at the well balancing the bucket,
always about to meet it, lip to lip.

Leaving the Shades Up

In the long twilights of November,
both evenings and mornings,
I like the shades up.
I like to see the gray world
looking in at my looking out.
I like to watch
the slow balancing of light
inside the house and out:
the shy stars returning,
becoming public, or fading
into the daylight sky
as when death came
to my father's eye.

Ultrasound
March 18, 2003

What trouble are you saved, small spirit?—
wavering there in the amniotic water,
scarcely realer than a dream
that bursts like a bubble in the morning light.

But you will never be abandoned to strangers
in a schoolroom, never venture, clutching
books and lunch, into the teeth of the world.
You won't know the flower of loss
when the buds of your breasts push at your shirt.
You are spared haphazards—
finding a work, a friend, a mate
whose demons don't inflame your own.
You will not end, my almost girl, where
your mother is, trying through acid tears
to divine the dark you rock in. Wrapped
in their black cocoon, your chromosomes,
your ventricles, your rank neural tube
echo the probings of the ultrasound.
The only answer is your mother's anguish.
Although you'll never swim into the world's
light, neither will your small, dark floating
bring you here: to joy's foreclosure
                    to such blind choosing.

Aubade

    April 2, 2003

Awakening in the half-dark
I heard the lovely cry of a bird, six notes
over and over, moving farther and farther away,
like a seed never burst,
a bud never bloomed,
like a flag ever furled.
Then day broke all across the town,
and the first sun of morning
scored the roofs and eaves of houses.

To My Grandson, in the Womb, on Washington Heights

I lie on my back in Kentucky summer grass,
my hat over my face, carried toward sleep
by the narcotic sunlight
and the cicadas' antiphonies.
In this bright little darkness
my eyes sting

picturing you cupped safely
in Lucy's belly, she in the sensible
shoes, since she snagged her high heel
and pitched to her knees in the street.
How strange you are,
hidden, distant, other,
carried on your own tide of blood,
grown from an egg into
the changeling the ultrasound reveals.

Here in this stillness, a mower
burrs on the next farm,
and in the lake a fish jumps.
But underneath your house the subway
rumbles like a troll, shaking already
the jelly of your bones.
Along for the ride, on weekday mornings
you board the "A" train for Times Square.
I fear for you in that pell-mell
as never for my daughters. Someday
an Agamemnon might summon you to arms;
enemies may fix you in their crosshairs, you
without even bones to speak of!
I pray that you will not be flung
from your proud city's heights, burst
like Hector's baby in the dust
beneath the walls of conquered Troy.

From this day-terror I am roused
by hoofbeats on the ground I lie upon.
I fling my hat aside and, dazzled by the sun,
make out a buck with half-grown antlers
dancing toward me; at my eruption
he turns to stone. The sunlight showers
around him. His dark eyes surge and deepen
before he rears, whirls, and rumbles back
into the shadows, parrying the sword of light.

Skating

> *Family:* that mysterious collection of ghosts
>   which, sooner or later, we become to each other;
>   some, shades we never knew,
>   others, shadows of those we loved the most.
>   —The Metaphysician's Dictionary

We move around the rink,
riding the waves of the organ's pulse,
under the sun of the spinning glory ball
showering particles of light alike upon
        the graceful dancers and the lame,
        who, limbs flailing, are carried
        willy-nilly against the flow,
        comical as the top-hatted man
        on the banana peel.

When the music slows, we
        stumble over the lip of the ice
        into the dark surround, out of
the cascading shards of light,
and, tipping our blades,
stagger toward a resting place, collapse,
looking back at our own, both gliders and duffers,
like pictures on black pages in an album.

Hidden there in the darkness,
we building, brick by brick,
a palace made of light,
where all is enfolded, a Heaven
        shaped like an egg
        where the skaters float
        uncertain and harmonious,
        like subatomic particles.

Your Company

for Aunt Mary
    (March 3, 1910–January 29, 2002)

Breathing to the rhythm of your breaths
(they cackle loudly in your throat),
no point to being here except being
here with you still being.
Such peaceful moments
when I sit beside the dying
whose lives have made my own.
You are here. I am here. For now, what else
is there? What is there to want except
the long ribbon of the past
scrolling to the end of itself?

Sitting with Aunt Mary in Hospice

> An eye that opens and then closes—
> Such is the life that seems endless to thee.
>
> —*Frithjof Shuon, "The Eye"*

My daughter sits beside your bed,
her fresh skin stretched full of herself,
her hair fanned on her shoulders, an aureole
under the hum of the fluorescent lamp.
On the bed, you are a husk from which
the seed has blown, your hair unruly
as old grass, your breath, a loud suspense,
and then another. Your eyes, part open,
clouded, still seem to see
me clearly. In them I see your wordless
grief and longing, and, astonished, see
my daughter in a body ruined as yours,
far past my care and comfort.
I accept that in an ever-nearer future
I will lie as you do, but I can't conceive
that her child's body, too, will
one day loosen on its rack of loss.
The river of days already carries me
off, but you and she are still borne up
out of this drowning on the flood
of my swelling, useless love.

The Reading Lamp

On Grandfather's eighty-eighth birthday
his children gave him a reading lamp,
which he trained on the newspaper
morning and evening. Sleek,
silver, modern, taller
than I was, it rose from the floor
on its leaden base. Its bulb
burned in the chromium shell
at the end of its gooseneck,
which my cousin and I bent
into snake shapes, scaring each other.

On the shell a gold sticker glistened,
embossed with a name,
a brand I can't remember.
Whom shall I ask?
Grandfather died the next year.
Aunt Grace died early of a stroke.
Aunt Mabel and Uncle Teddy,
of lung cancer. My father,
my mother, both gone. My cousin,
too—a suicide.

I alone have lived to tell this
little story, and now I approach
the dark to which they've gone.
A last hope, that lamp
still shines, like silver,
gold, a wondrous light
which won't yet yield its name.

Eating a Pear from the Tree My Father Planted Thirty-One Years Ago

> For God so loved the world that he gave his only begotten son,
> that whosoever believeth in him should . . . have everlasting life.
>
> —*John 3:16*

One hand still on the shovel he's used
to plant in his garden this pear tree,
an apple, and a peach, he wanted his
picture taken with the three saplings,
his two grandchildren, and the shovel.
What is he seeing as he gazes proudly,
more at the children than the trees?
Granted he foresees this moment
when the tree's strong spine holds
up a universe of golden, tempting orbs,
now about to shower down
upon the earth. He sees, I hope, beyond
his cancer, beyond his sorrows
for his children, past the future hurts
of the babies with him there, to this
far-off fall with its unlikely bounty.
Though the peach and apple withered
(sometimes the fate of virtue),
this great floozy of a pear
outlived him, and the sprout
that touched his hip is now
at least ten times his height,
its limbs so thick
they could be trees themselves.

This year the summer started early
(no late frost), was cool throughout,
replete with rain, and now the fall
stays cool but long, with no hard frost.
The pears have formed at every nodule
on this tree, at every notch where, back
in May, outpourings of white flowers
foreshadowed this. For two months

now the windfall has been greater than
the usual whole yield, and still
they're falling in the fertile circle
underneath the tree, so hard and fast
they come that they have pulled down
three big branches, loaded still, upon
the ground. I hope he's seeing this
October day of sky electric blue,
the heft of this gold sunset light.
Perhaps he knows the earnest hearts,
and hard, brave growth of the two
children beside him there, shading
their eyes from the sun that fell
that day on their brown shoulders,
thrown back in pride that they
had helped him plant these trees.

He planted trees, so enacting
his love and deep connection
to the world. He had Mother take
this picture so that a moment of beginning
might persist. For my own part,
here alone where his garden used to be,
seeing the many bushels of pears still
clinging after many weeks, still falling
(though several neighbors have
pear jelly on their shelves), regarding
the broken elbows of the limbs
that couldn't hold such flourishing,
I see the perfect figure for his heart:
a pear that I pick up, not bruised
from its long fall, not broken open,
not yet a sweetmeat at this harvest feast,
not sipped at by drunken hornets,
or gorged upon by jays, not burrowed in
by bees, nor fed upon by sluggish snakes,
without bite marks of coons or possums,
but shining in its globular perfection,
so winsome in its rusty wholesomeness
that I take its rough skin to my lips
and crack its flesh upon my teeth.

One Summer in the Life of My Mother

> I have Three Treasures which I hold fast and watch over closely. The first is *Mercy*. The second is *Frugality*. The third is *Not Daring to Be First in the World*. Because I am frugal, therefore I can be generous. Because I dare not be first, therefore I can be the chief of all vessels.
>
> —Tao Teh Ching, *No. 67*

I came upon the book again when I was cleaning out
the desk where she paid bills and kept farm records:
a calendar book, four days to the double page,
where she logged the events of summer 1958,
before my high school senior year. She wrote
on June 22, "Dear Jane,—I'm going to try to write
in this book everything that happens at home
so you can read it when you're back from France."
It was the first time I'd been away so long.
She was forty-four, with amber hair
and creamy skin, and on October pages
in the back, after summer days had petered out,
she listed in neat columns all the calories she ate
for several weeks on her reducing diet,
always with dessert at lunch and supper.
The days she noted here for me
are like a string of crystal beads, each full of light,
one scarcely different from the rest. She worked
hard, but each day brought pleasures: June 23,
a Monday, always wash day: "Washed—
took Charlie to his baseball game (Rebels 10—
Senators [his team]—4). C.B. involved in barley.
Had supper at 8 o'clock—read magazine—
at home and early to bed." That one word *washed*
belies her single-handed hauling
of the spin-dryer from underneath the stairs,
the difficult attachment of the hoses to the faucets
in the kitchen sink, and the hanging of a half-dozen
heavy loads of shirts, jeans, underwear,
khakis, and bedclothes on the backyard line.

But then the pleasure of a baseball game, making
a little supper, reading *Collier's* in the easy chair,
and up to bed by ten, without need to accomplish
beyond the day, nor any worry for tomorrow.

Only phrases here and there admit of any feeling.
Two days after my departure she wrote: "Up at six
so C.B. could get to the barley. I did nothing today
but mess around and read. Mrs. Setzer called tonight
and said somebody's father in New York
went to the pier, and saw you board your ship.
I was *sure* glad to hear even indirectly.
It's a funny feeling to think about you out
on the ocean and not be able to know
if you are sick or well, happy or sad—"
But her writing was not shaded; rather was
a useful record of life lived within its limits,
an accounting she made to save for me
that summer's slow days in their flow.
Four or five nights a week they played rum,
six- or nine-card, or bridge, all for fun,
spiced by the modest sums they wagered.
They played with sisters and brothers-in-law,
with friends and cousins, who were also neighbors,
with Old Boy, my father's cousin, old enough
to be his father, who lived back in the fields
alone, a rich man, whose black pick-up was
ramshackle as he, his clothes held on with pins.
Mother kept a tally of how much she won:
Thursday, June 26: "Raining—Richard came in
and talked to me till Charlie got up—made some
potato salad & cooked green beans—called
Miss Mary Farney and fixed her a box of quilt pieces.
C.B. went to town. Charlie went to work
with Richard and his father this afternoon.
Six-card rum at Mabel and Tom's. + $5.00."

The rightness of these days rings true, no sense
of over-doing, even on the big day, July Fourth:
"10:50 a.m. Dear Jane, I miss you. I have just

finished frying chicken, making lemonade
for our all-day picnic—just my family—Nice day—
talked and ate. Charlie built a pony cart. The Allisons
brought the pup back. Everyone gone by 9 p.m.—"
after the last Roman candle exploded from its bottle.

The next day, a Saturday, she checked rain
on the daily weather grid: "Cleaned up from the 4th—
Pony League picnic—real nice. Charlie didn't go
so we came home early. Mary and Dav, Mabel
and Tom, Old Boy played 6-card rum till 1 o'clock—
−50 cents." Only three times all summer long does
she mention television, and then it's always
"Watched the Reds game on tv tonight."

In the back of the book, on pages for addresses,
she listed and crossed off chores remaining
in her yearly house cleaning, top to bottom.
"Upstairs—wash windows and hang curtains
washroom. Downstairs—hall—wash woodwork,
clean lights, wax floor—" and so for all the rooms.
She'd learned industry from her mother, but her days
were pleasureful: along with work of meals
and house, time for reading, napping, baseball,
playing cards, eating out at Jerry's or at Smoot's.
Her days were rich with people. No society as such,
but ample daily comfort of connection, talking
with her mother and her sisters on the phone
("Hello, what are you doing?"), visiting neighbors,
the ritual banter at card tables in the evenings.
On Wednesday, July 9: "Jane's first letter from France
came this morning. She ate an artichoke
in Deauville. Dovie was here and we cleaned
the kitchen. Richard ate supper with us. Mrs. Livesay
called and told me about her letters from Jo Ann.
Hogs are better. Went to Mabel and Tom's tonight
and stayed till 12. Charlie B. won $11.00. Rain."
The last day of writing, she figured totals
for three months: "from May 3 to August 4,
6-card +$22.50—9-card +$105.80." Nobody

else kept track, knew how consistently she won,
or guessed how much she relished winning.

What does this add up to? Not a remarkable life,
by standards of achievement, but still a wonder
of easeful time, mid-span, her children half-grown,
moving in their own directions, I, the older,
even on another continent. Simple routines
of cooking that didn't seem a burden, the cycle
of wash days and cleaning house in company
with Dovie. She accommodated Daddy's
movements and farm work: feeding the hogs
after supper, going to the stockyards
every week, seeing to the barley and the hay,
his several daily stops at the crossroads store
in Athens, buying bread, picking up the evening paper.
There were sadnesses and trials,
but they were short and trivial in 1958:
the luckless Senators didn't win a single game
all summer, though Charlie got his hits.
And on the last page of the book she sketched
the floor plan of the house she wanted, new
and ordinary, still five years away, without
the twelve-foot ceilings of this lovely,
too-big house of the peaceful summer
that I missed, that she wrote down for me.
It was a Golden Age, but, as ages go,
scarcely there, tipping in the balance:
past were my father's chicken-fighting
days and all-night drinking binges.
She had told him after years of pleading
that if he left again he'd come back
to find her gone, but us still there for him
to raise. Yet to come were her own sorrows,
a list not long, not extraordinary:
her parents died as she of course expected,
Charlie's head was broken in a wreck,
a long, slow cancer took her Charlie B.,
her sister Mildred died suddenly, too early,
Charlie's wound festered in his children.

Her heart broke, cracked the dam that kept
her sorrow in. Her dementia came on
fast, flooding out 1958, along with all
her other seasons. But because she wrote
this book, that summer isn't gone.
Here and now I read between her penciled lines
her mother's hope that I, though still a child,
would know her in a future which she could not
guess, as she was that almost perfect summer,
when my absence just rehearsed the losses
yet to come, a moment in her life of the best
that we can hope for: bright as the burning
of a July day, warm as the light of amber hair,
brief and brilliant as the summer sky.

Three

Portrait of the Artist as a White Pig

At sunset on a November day, the world unrolls
itself beside the Western Kentucky Parkway.
Gilded in sunlight, bronze as a baby shoe,
the dead leaves burn on the trees, red, gold,
black, spread rich as an Oriental rug.
Green flames of side-lit cedars burnish all.

Then, over the short horizon appears the hero,
alien as brontosaurus, strange,
but of a multitude: white pigs,
a field full, eating, all snouts
to the ground they've rooted up, plowed
like furrows in the cognac-colored light.
That earth should take the form of this
strange beast, should eat itself and shift
into this shape! The bows of their backs
gold-leafed: snout and mouth to golden earth,
as hungry as one breath for the next.
Unnatural as Midas' kingdom
in the sideways sun, what other
brutes could translate this
bright dirt? This heavy
light? These showers of gold?

At Pleasant Hill, Kentucky, in January

    (Shaker Village, restored 1964)

A day so cold my car tires roll like rocks
along the road. In the fields, only the cedar
trees seem at home in the ice-bright air.
My garret room high in the East Family House
has two plain windows, the only decoration
on the walls. In the upper sash, a wan blue
January sky hazy with crystalline veils.

In the lower sash, a drift of furnace steam,
birds riding by like sentences across my thoughts.
A nuthatch and a flicker scour a locust
for whatever mites survive this cold.
A chickadee levitates branch to branch.
Ever-indignant crows voice their complaints.
And on the ground, no Shakers, but family
groups of sightseers: an antic roly-poly child,
grandfather in a Scottish cap, stolid
parents slung with cameras and packs,
grandmother picking her way upon the icy path.

Then the music of a train. I can see it
over the white humpback hills, through fencerows
of naked trees along the umber skyline. It
stitches in and out of sight, blasts its horn again
at High Bridge crossing the Kentucky River.
Small as toys, its coal cars crawl, straightforward
as shoelaces, toward Dix Dam.

A weekend visitor, I am at home
in this resurrected village, this frozen
countryside, in which my mother was a child
just beyond the far-off tracks, in Wilmore,
where her grandmother grew up, too,
on this home ground
where I've never spent a night before.

Once every place but home was foreign, but home now
widens, becomes stranger than I thought possible. Here
in Shakertown I sleep like a baby on its mother's lap.
From my gable window I see dawn come
across the rim of the horizon, an orange
gash through which new daylight pours.

Taking the Train from Maysville to New York

    September 11, 2002

Leaving Versailles at 4 a.m., only a glint of light
in the east. The stars so quiet. One watching
above the gable of my house, close as in childhood.
On the drive to Maysville, just a handful of cars
on the country highways. Out the window I see
the gauze of the Milky Way unrolled across the sky.
The Dipper so clear, dot to dot. Orion lazy, low
to the horizon. Near Paris, the sheerest sliver
of the new moon raises the old above the trees.

Then on the train headed toward West Virginia,
running alongside the broad-bosomed Ohio,
the levee now gold in the rising sun,
farmsteads, entire cities of rolled hay,
power plants with smoke plumes blooming
into the pink sky, towns of vine-latticed houses
facing the tracks. Oh for the voice of Whitman
or Twain to catalog these visions of America
framed by the train window, much as they lay
150 years ago. Through the dappled
trees yellowed in sun, I see the mist, the lovely
breath of the Ohio rising in shafts, alive, inviting
rest, but my sleep-heavy eyes won't close out
the sun blazing its pathway on the river.

The rails sing a low, syncopated song.
The coach cradles me and rocks across small rivers
and large, past cornfields tasseled out, past
vine-wrapped barns, square bales of scrap metal
heaped beside the tracks outside of Ashland,
past two women visiting on a narrow plant-filled
porch, past the aquamarine geometries of backyard pools,
past herds of cattle, heads down, shadows humped,

indefinite, wrenching up the generosities of grass
far, far yet from the city once innocent of its riches,
its towering heights, which now knows, like its poor sisters
all across the earth, the fist out of the sky, the shock,
the fire, the smoke-choked darkness, and descent.

The Light at the End of the Tunnel

Is this a poem that should be written?
I stand looking out the back window
of the last car of the train.

It has emerged from the darkness
of the tunnel into blinding sunlight.
I watch the track inexorably narrow
into a straight line behind us, finally
disappearing into the black mouth
we've just come out of.
Smaller and smaller, the doorway of light
at the other end of the tunnel.

Utopia: An Idyll

Everyone in the Utopia Diner seems happy:

the regulars who, in the middle of the afternoon,
wander in; the Greek waiters standing at their posts
joshing each other, all in short-sleeved
white shirts and slick black ties; the proprietor
in his bright Polo, licking his thumb
behind the cash register, counting out
dollar bills to dishwashers and busboys
changing shifts. He dispenses money
with equanimity, just as he takes it in.
One waiter lines up all the ketchup bottles
and pours the almost empty into the almost
full, until each table has a fresh, new bottle.

In the booth next to mine, two teenage girls
 (known to the younger waiters, who smilingly
bring them extra fries, refill their cokes)
lean toward each other, whispering, in their
low-cut jeans and high-cut shirts, the skin
of their hips and waists glowing against
the leather of the banquette. An old couple
of familiars, he in a Yankees cap, she with
a Greek sailor hat upon her too-bright auburn
hair, order carefully, negotiating a split
of the three-egg, two-waffle breakfast
available twenty-four seven.

My eggs arrive exactly as I want them,
scrambled hard, with two twists of bacon
crisp and overcooked. On this November day
my decaf with skim milk, poured over
and over into my never-empty cup,
is ichor in my veins in Utopia, the diner.

Rose Week in the Brooklyn Botanic Garden

> And what is so rare as a day in June?
> Then, if ever, come perfect days.
>
> —*James Russell Lowell*

A gull like a paper plane
sails high on a blue current
over the garden gate where
a rose drops its red vestments
into the bloody puddle of a birdbath.
The traffic soughs, then
hushes, growls again.
Overhead, a sky out of childhood—
the country of clouds real as continents.
The air, sweet as a blossom.

Under their tiny backpacks, schoolgirls
in skirts below their knees straggle
along the path behind their teacher
in her oxfords and her headscarf.
They look back open-mouthed
at the old woman scribbling on a pad
and sitting cross-legged on forbidden grass.

The roses, two days past their prime,
still yawn and flirt. They have
their moment, after all. This is
as real as death, this silkiness,
these many-colored petals,
curling at the lip. The brilliance
of the Pearly Gates! The scent
of crimson at Life's Fountain!
Oh how sheer the Angel Tears!
The jumbo Grand Hotel entwined
with sunny Dainty Bess! At the bottom
of the garden, the purple thunder
roll of Distant Drums!

In the reflecting pool, two dragonflies doubled
careen in tandem like fighter jets refueling.
In Cherry Lane, a young mother, still egg-bellied,
drops on all fours beside her infant lying
on its stomach in the grass. Crisp in white
the baby spasms like a beached fish,
and the mother laughs her delight, all teeth,
inches from the baby's velvet face.

On the Eve of War with Iraq
March 17, 2003

Safe at home today, making my rounds
to the grocery, my office, the cleaners,
reading, preparing classes for tomorrow,
I think of those on the other side of the world
who might not be alive tomorrow—
boys and girls the age of those I teach,
costumed in camouflage and khaki,
ranged at the borders with gas masks and guns.

And in Iraqi villages and cities, fathers,
sons, grandmothers, mothers, soldiers
ply their routines at home,
getting their children dressed and fed,
laying in food and water, boarding windows,
cleaning weapons, awaiting the attack
the others poise for.

Perhaps Heaven is earth
without the water of blood,
air without the song of breath,
for every heart clutches at its own blood.
We know the fire will fall—we hope
on someone else, on someone else's
children, someone else's house—out
of the blank sky, the blind eye of the sun.

My Two Daughters in Paris

What pleasure it gives me to think of them
walking the leafy streets, the sunny quais, arm in arm
along the generous boulevards, looking for the right
table under the trees for a drink, or their supper.

I see them in les Jardins du Luxembourg looking
into the cool length of the Medici Fountain, then
on the gravelly terrace, their backs to the shadows
of the grove. They sit close under the stony gazes
of les reines de la France. In the distance, along
the pool's shimmer, their remnant childhood
dreams unfurl in patches of bright flowers.

The best of what they have from me is their being
in this tapestry, no forgotten pins, needles biting
through the fabric, as in the mother spell I weave.

When finally we say good-bye, whether I'm the traveler
or they, unthinkably, are leaving me, this temptation
I will cling to: the vision of two sisters in a garden,
the music of a strange tongue in their mouths, sun
gilding their hair, each head inclined toward the other,
hearts blooming, yearning toward all the earth holds out.

Nike of Samothrace

All victory is winged. Goddess, you
lean forward from the prow of your ship,
the folds of your chiton swept back
by the wind you ride upon at the top
of the main stairway in the Louvre.
You took this form in a lost town
on an Aegean island where husbands
gossiped and bartered in the agora,
and wives busied themselves in the dark rooms
of their houses, hearing the slap of men's
feet on the paving stones. Near the harbor
in a work-shed veiled in dust, you rose up
plane by plane, in the mind's eye
of a stonecutter, who, over years,
laboriously discovered you, chip
by chip, inside the body of a stone.

When at last he finished nicking, filing,
polishing, giving you the final caresses
of shapeliness, could he remember, any more
than we, the victory you commemorate?
For now you are Victory, the ache
of exultation, no sooner felt than gone.

You bear into the wind always
your wings of stone
spread to catch the lift of air.
And deep in your rocky bones
a Thracian breeze still blows,
exciting your fleshy nipple
under the wind-sheered cloth.
Tides of people swell around
the bow of your broken ship.
The lightning of their cameras
fixes you time and again

in the chiffon of winning. Your torso,
robust as the sea wind pushing you,
torques against all that is fleet.
You stretch back against these currents
the feathery stone of your resisting wings.

Les Jardins du Luxembourg

In the vista of the Queens of France we sit.
The fountains spill
onto the pool's green, moving mirror.
On the terrace, the rows of plane trees
burgeon in the sun.
The palm fronds agitate
as in a tropic breeze.
Within the grove, the shadow opens
a dark inviting room
into which a runner disappears,
and a woman pushing a blue stroller,
and two young men bent forward from their backpacks,
and an old man with a newspaper under his arm.

A gardener with bronze legs
bends, trims the border of a border.

Leaving the Sidewalk Café

Overhead, crows squabble and parry
as I walk away from the restaurant where
glad voices rise and fall, riding the surf
of syntax, sentences in counterpoint
to sentences, cresting as they would have
to the ears of a Minoan lady pausing
on the Great Staircase to listen to
the cadences of talk at the banquet
she had left, or to a Neolithic woman
stopped in the cave mouth to hear her clan
feasting on a kill around the nightly fire.

I look back at the awning strung
with lights, and hear the sharp tattoos
of forks and knives against the plates.
No great occasion, only friends
in company eating together, all safe
for now from perils (the lightning strike,
the wind's maw, the worm of poison)
and threats (the loved body stiff as a claw),
while abiding harmonies of conversation
over food rise into the evening air
amid the ancient discords of the crows.

Portrait of Sue Richards as a Young Girl

> Because it was a woman
> Who built a house for death
> A shining girl tore it down.
>
> —*Hildegard of Bingen*

See her now as she was then,
in the over-ripe Eden of central Florida,
a girl of eight or nine, skinny, tanned,
flint-eyed, shinnying up the tree, limb
over limb, as if there were stair steps
among the leathery leaves of the magnolia.
Slaphappy, giddy with daring, hell-bent
on the fiery fruit at the tip of a branch,
she doffs and bobs above the innocents
below, faces upturned, mouths agape.
"The world tree is blossoming. Two
realms become one. . . .
Never was leaf so green . . . ,"
never so white the last bloom
she passes on her way,
fragrant as the queen's perfume,
purest vessel, round as a plate,
luminous as the moon.
She stops and meets the flower
lip to lip, drunk
on the glory of high heaven.

The Clouds, My Mother

Windermere Island, Eleuthera, the Bahamas

The white clouds on the horizon
billow against the blaze of sky.
Out on the water, I see the manes
of the breakers, then the clear aquamarine
where we swim, and beyond the reef
the black water where the barracuda,
amberjack, and tuna live in their imageless
world. On shore, the rapiers of palmetto
fronds under the morning sun,
the pastel houses set in dunes,
and, in the sand, footprints
of a cat and her four kittens, hieroglyphs
of a language lost in this sea place.
Almost unseen at home, the clouds
here fill the eye in their entirety, schooners
swelling, making for the verge.

Watching Stars

Eleuthera juts like an elbow
from the dark sea.
We lie on the warm sand
and watch for falling stars.
And what is one, or two,
or three, among the countless
brilliants that we see?
And yet their light is black.
I cannot see my hand
six inches from my eyes.

Behind us in the foliage
chameleons have turned black.
They flick from frond to frond,
and climb the spines of leaves.
Light years ago, these lights
we see tonight were buried
in the stars, and the sly lizards
with their lidless eyes
and traceries of bone bore
the weight of tyrannosaur.

Parable of the Reverse Sunset

We sit transfixed in the dusk, as if chained
in our chairs, the fire behind us, looking
at the eastern sky for the whole half-hour of sunset,
watching the sea and clouds shift, reflections
of each other. Patterns of light glisten,
tumble together (pink, red, lavender,
purple, black) like pieces in a kaleidoscope.
In the clouds we see shapes: a cat's head, a horsefly,
the outline of Kentucky, a baby sucking its thumb.
With all the pleasure of vacancy, far from our cares,
we watch this strangeness as if we might learn
something useful from such slantwise vigilance
(the luxury of looking where the action isn't),
something the direct, revolutionary Plato didn't.

First Kiss

We said good-bye standing at my car.
Your tongue was sly as an inside joke.

When I wiped my lipstick off your lips,
my fingers read the Braille of my longing,
an old alphabet, signs of a lost language.

April in Your Garden

The day falls open out of the sky.
Even the cedar bent from the wet late snow
seems to rise up into it
like the richest voice in a chorus.

Your body is as real as a tree.
I sit outside in bright sunshine
and see your movements tap like a ghost
behind the screen of the open window.

My hand gripping this pen
suddenly yearns toward home: between
your neck and shoulder, inside
the glove of your hand—places right

as the purse of the oriole's nest
I see rising, falling on invisible
currents high in the ash tree,
among green fists of new leaves.

Nearby

I doze on a bench in a garden.
Like a cat, I absorb June sunshine.
A bird dips so close I hear its bony
whir. My eyes open a slit. A butterfly
sips at a bloom that bobs under the tissue
of its wings. In the flowery light
my open book warms on my chest. A cardinal
pours out the syrup of its song. The pinks
throb in the still-cool air. A bee
forces the nod from a head of clover.
I sit up then, and see
nearby on the meadow grass
a hawk's shadow sailing in circles.

By Your Small Lake

At dusk I sit in the leftover sunshine
your dock absorbed this July day.
The gray boards, familiar as an old
blanket, practical as a spoon,
bring to mind your hands: warm, dry,
wise as a toolbox. The bourbon
you brought me smolders in my throat
sharpens my focus on a tableau
across the lake: many turtles, one
upon the other, heaped like rocks
on a tree trunk fallen
in the water off the far bank.
In the shallows near my feet, a carp,
cross-hatched, thick as a club,
whips to the surface for an insect,
breaks the dark back of the green
mirror, raising a chocolate cloud
from the lake's bottom. Startled,
an invisible frog grumps once
and, through the blackening surface, drops
like the pancakes your deft hands turned
this morning as you made breakfast—
your hands which wavered all night
over the lake of my body, its dark
mirroring our hungers rising
cunning as the turtles, shining
as the fish, to feed.

At Harmony Landing

> I never had a patient who spent part of
> his day looking over water.
>
> *—Sigmund Freud*

I am reading on the porch above the lake.
Cicadas are singing.
Now and again a breeze stirs the air.
I lift my eyes from my story,
and see, on the green water, circles
running outward from a center.

Immersed in words again, I hear a cry
or a double splash, or a thump
against the barrels of the dock,
but I never catch the fish
in air, the bird mid-dive,
or see the frog jump.

Still, the rings widen
into calm, their center fathomless.

Penelope's Night Out

Last night the fall crescent drifted down a summer sky.
The crickets sang their eternal one-note chorus.
You and I went to a party in a lovely room filled
with likenesses of the hosts in the beauty
of their youth, and with the books they cherish.
The room opened to a porch that gave upon a woods.
I watched its stand of handsome tree trunks fade
in the twilight. I chatted up a temptress in whose thrall
you once were held. After we drained the sweet liquor
from the last cubes in our glasses, we said good-bye
to friends, and to the pleasant new acquaintances.

We stepped into a moonless darkness and drove,
companionably touching hands, thighs in the golden light
of the dashboard. At home, we stepped out of our clothes
and laughed again at a conversation I had overheard.
We spoke, too, of Calypso's presence there. Then
as we lay beside each other, sleepily touching, with our
mouths, our fingers, our viscous skin, a wakefulness
surprised us like a wave, rolled us into the ecstasy
of this unlikely night, and dropped us, sleeping
soundly as you did, Odysseus, surrounded by all
your treasure, on the strange shore of home.

Sleeping with You

We climb onto the motorcycle of sleep.
I flatten myself against your back,
lock one arm around your waist,
and off we roar toward the rallies of night,
the marks of all our years streaming behind
us, like my white silk scarf rippling, useless,
riding the black wind.

The Traveler

I

A mile above the bony reach of trees, I doze
in a silver capsule skimming peaks of clouds.
The tiny egg of comfort I have swallowed
suspends my phobias, and, happy
as a baby on its mother's shoulder, lulled
by the uplift of the engines,
I come face to face with what I own and am,
with what I'm all but ready to surrender:

if all happinesses are not mine,
well, neither are all the sorrows.

Then, my adenoidal flutter jerks me
awake, saliva on my chin.
My furtive eyes open straight into the gaze
of the matron in Italian shoes across the aisle.

II

The joy of my face nicked by winter wind;
the joy of my legs, each swinging one foot
in front of the other on the dark sidewalk;
the joy of my eyes feasting on spun sugar
clouds afloat with the half-moon
above the towers of the glittering city;
the joy of my shoulders weighed down
by my packages and bag of books:

how few of us are lucky enough to live
the life we're prepared for,

even for moments at a time, not deploying
the divisions of our body into foreign struggles,
but fitting our life like moss fits the trees
the plane passed over at such improbable heights.

The Chain: A True Account

(Mary House Gentry, 1870–1952)

Mary seldom smiled, except to laugh,
and usually to herself, on dappled porches
where she sat all summer making something
from nothing, fancywork quilts from feed sacks
and old georgette; aprons from worn-out dresses;
doorway chains from empty thread spools;
socks she'd knitted long ago, she darned
now for the third time, or the fourth.
Such thrift was what was left of her religion.
As she worked, she sang like a cat purrs,
from underneath her throat, "Amazing Grace,"
"She Was Only a Bird in a Gilded Cage,"
or "Arkansas Traveler," all the verses
Uncle George brought back from Oregon.
Her eyes lifted sometimes, empty,
from her sewing. Her voice still singing,
she lost herself in shifting puzzles
of the light. She'd loved her mother, Martha,
dead at fifty-two, beneath the burden
of her husband's restlessness; Mary mourned
Paulina, oldest sister, tubercular at twenty;
and sickly Hiram, sweetest baby, dead
at eight, and as she stitched there on the porch,
her body felt the heaviness of walking through
the clinging grasses of the summer field
toward the shady rock-walled graveyard
at White's Station where her dead lie now
so far from home listening, she thinks,
for the whistle of the selfsame train that brought
them hopeful, seeking, from the mountains.

Or she laughed telling her husband Pick again,
or a sister, or one of her seven children,
a puzzle or a joke enjoyed many times before,
old stories of people they had known,

or known about, being strong or weak
or foolish, back in the mountains
or at White's Station, where they were
strangers for the first time in their lives.
Her favorite story was on herself.
In 1916 an earnest drummer found her full
of pride in her new house, its dining room
so big that all the children sat with her
and Pick around the claw-foot table.
So handsome the peddler selling dishes—
a big Blue Willow platter caught her eye.
It was unbreakable, he said, was more
than worth the seven dollars he was asking.
How it matched her Sunday dishes! Over
and over he let it fall, and it stayed whole
as a silver dollar, while in its glaze shone
the three Chinamen always crossing
the bridge; it easily would hold the meat
of four fried chickens. But the tobacco crop
was only just now set, the Prewitt Place's
mortgage soon was due. She always saved
her egg and cream money for the children's
new school shoes. But finally, she pulled
the jam jar off the back shelf in the pantry,
and bought herself a brand-new egg-shaped
platter tied with twine in its own box.
At suppertime her family filled their plates,
and she brought out the big surprise she'd promised.
The children held their breath, were saucer-eyed
at the huge blue-pictured oval of it.
"This platter will not break," she swore to them,
"no matter how it falls." She dropped it then.
It shattered in an awful silence.
One stunned second, and she commenced to laugh
until hard tears flowed down her face. Teddy
set up a wail among the solemn children.
"Pride goeth before a fall," she said
through laughter. Long after, for her
and for her children, that plate remained
the emblem of the danger of desire.

At three o'clock on those long summer days
she took her basket and her needlework
into the dark, cool hallway, where she sat,
head bowed before the console radio,
and soared and wept with "Stella Dallas"
till time to feed the hens and gather eggs.

In 1900 when they married, Pick was forty.
Old maid at thirty, Mary had already lived
another life, not the eldest daughter,
but the smartest and the prettiest, born
on Rockcastle River in Kentucky mountains
that hemmed her father in, kept him always
uprooting them, seeking his fortune, first in
the foothills near Berea at White's Station.
But he aimed ever toward the promised land,
the Bluegrass, where always the next farmstead,
the next town, the next crossroads store would make
of Thomas House a prosperous man, would make
his family healthy, happy. They grew to twelve.
Out by the roots Thomas pulled them, over
and over, just as they got to know the teacher
at whatever country schoolhouse, and got
longed-for invitations to the neighbors' dances.

At thirteen, Mary's hands were red
from scalding diapers, and she was deft,
but not so gentle, at tucking shirttails,
wiping noses of the little ones. Martha,
overwhelmed, grew weak and sickened,
while more and more Tom left bright Mary, good
at numbers and with customers, to keep
the store while he went fishing, set tobacco,
played nine-card rum, or tended to his hounds.
At White's Station, then at Poosey Ridge,
at Paint Lick, and finally at Athens, the family
half grown now, he thought he'd found
at last the land of milk and honey: white
clapboard cottage with pretty gingerbread;
the big high-ceilinged store with walnut shelves

and tin-topped counter; rich bottomland
to rent; and the relief and gratitude
of law-abiding citizens that this strange
mountain man would try to keep the peace
in Athens, a still unruly frontier town.
Elected magistrate, Tom was the only man
among the neighbors brave enough, or fool
enough, to want the job. He was policeman,
jury, judge, and jailer all in one.

And Mary kept the books, knew how much flour
to trade for pecks of wormy apples, rusty
pole beans, knew how to keep the men from
dipping in the cracker barrel, spitting
on the stove, loafing too long on the porch.
She collected all accounts, even Robert Martin's
and Maybelle Short's, hard cases Tom had given up.
She was courted by the bravest bachelors in the county,
the few not cowed by her straight eyes,
her honest tongue: the doctor from Virginia
and the prosperous keeper of the rival store.
But at thirty, her mother dead, her sisters grown
and caring for the little ones, she chose a poor man,
Pick, soon richer than the others all combined.
He labored in tobacco, in his cattle
for fourteen hours a day when light was long.
And this she liked—she was a worker, too.
He'd sworn he'd never marry till he owned
a farm himself, expected hands he hired
(both white and black) for fifty cents a day
to work as hard as he did for himself.
At forty, he had his farm at last, had found
this stern and queenly maid who suited him
exactly. Too peculiar to dismount and come
inside to court, he sat upon his horse
across the road whenever time allowed,
for three long years, in winter and in summer,
his favorite hound, Old Thunder, asleep
at Traveler's feet, and waited for some business
to bring his Mary out of doors. She paid

him little mind, preferred the custom of her
father's store to choosing from among these men.

Ever restless, Thomas, missing Martha,
still not rich, but disillusioned, threatened
by a man he'd jailed, moved his worn-out
family one step back into the mountains.
Then Pick would ride all day to pay his court
at Sander's Ferry deep in Garrard County.
In June of 1900, in Thomas's dark parlor,
they married with the youngest children peeking
through the banisters. "Do you take this woman
to be your lawful wedded wife?" "Certainly,
certainly," answered Pick in the Virginia tones
he never lost. Next day, she rode with him
back into Athens, starting another life.

At thirty-one she started having babies,
more boys than girls, all sturdy, keen,
and definite as briars. None died until old age.
Pick delighted in them, having gone so long
without them, spoiled them, doomed them,
with her help, vowed he'd go on earning
Bluegrass farms until he got them one apiece.
And there was violence in it: Pick's nephew
Crazy Jim (Pick raised him from a boy) came
one morning, brandishing a knife, to play
with Charlie B. Her scared heart flamed as Jim's
empty blue eyes filled her own. She handed him
her baby, praying she would get him back alive.
All morning, from inside the darkness
of the kitchen, she watched, scarcely breathing,
shushing the others, frightened, too, as the man
and baby played beside the icehouse with the kittens.
At dinnertime, Jim handed Charlie B. inside
to her and took his own plate to the shade.

The many years of loss (her brother, mother,
sister) made it hard for her to give her love
its head, even to her children, always

wanting of her. But if she was not tender,
still she always tended them, and all her tasks:
her garden, turkeys, guineas, chickens.
She sold eggs and cream in town on Thursdays,
planted hollyhocks and roses by the cabin,
tiger lilies down the driveway lined with poplars,
always keeping careful records of what
she planted when and where, when she set
the guineas and the geese, when they hatched,
how many hatchlings lived. Each night
she took her diary from the chifforobe
beside the hearth and wrote about the weather,
who'd come to visit, which sons stayed out
all night the night before, and in the back
she kept a list of neighbors' deaths that year.

Once at dinner on a July afternoon
heavy with storm, with sixteen at her table
(the children, Pick, the threshers, and herself)
the kitchen cat, stealing Teddy's drumstick,
bit through the palm of his small hand. She rose,
staunched the baby's punctures, and then flung
the cat against the chopping block,
and with the axe chocked off his head
onto the woodpile and resumed her place
at table. When Grace, third oldest, Pick's
favorite, crept behind her rocking chair one day
and, thinking it a good joke on her mother,
pulled her somersaulting over backwards
with the baby, Mary snatched the buggy whip
and raised a single welt on Grace's
back that neither of them ever could forget.

At forty-four she said to Pick, "No more"
(three girls, four boys, all pretty, full of vim,
calling in the night, pulling at her apron,
wanting another biscuit, piece of chicken,
or needing a button or a patch). She ordered,
from Sears Catalogue, twin rosewood beds.
Outside the Blue Room where they slept, she nailed

a trace chain from her father's plowing harness.
When night winds swung it up against the boards,
its music brought back mountain days to her,
the red-roofed house beside Rockcastle River
where in 1893 her removal had begun.

When Pick was in bed, dying, he thought all
the years had folded back into their flower,
that he was at Belle Brezing's famous house
in Lexington. "Oh, please, don't tell Mary,"
he pleaded, raveling at the feed-sack quilt.
"Tell her I'll be home directly."

Older, Mary refused to set her foot
in Athens. Each Saturday, Jim Buck put on
a gold-braided chauffeur's cap and drove her
to the Jim Nix Cafeteria in Lexington.
Looking neither left nor right, she passed
the Athens crossroads, passed the store she used
to keep; dressed in black finery and gold beads,
she rode the long Queen Mary, her own Buick,
bought with her savings from her cream and fowl.
Then she felt rich beyond her father's dreams.

On these bright Saturdays as she leaves home,
she sometimes feels herself a girl again,
beside her mother on the wagon seat,
holding tight to skinny Hiram as they left
the red-roofed house beside Rockcastle River.
And she remembers how she looked back
from the last bend in the rutty road
through tears galling as her mother's,
until the trees obscured the white-washed house,
the red roofs of the farm where they were born,
Martha's dowry sold to stake them in the Bluegrass.

Finally, she can't believe her life has gone,
that Pick is dead. She sees her children's lives
convolute with trouble. She tells whoever listens,
"If I had it to do over, I wouldn't have a single child."

Puzzlement clouds her eyes with cataracts.
Small strokes dull her tongue. Her house is empty as
October sky. Beside the hearth, her jaw slacks;
she watches embers die. Sometimes she hears
her children's voices crying for a touch
she cannot give. Inside her chifforobe,
the five-year diaries press her days in locked-
up pages. In her balls of string, her rows
of canning jars, her boxes of old lace
and linens, articles of life all stacked
on shelves, arranged in drawers, in pantries,
her mind shifts, settles like motes in thick,
last rays of sun. Her white hair, like a dandelion,
seems to froth as she nods in her chair.
Her thoughts soon drift away. Dark winds
will lift her memories, seed by weightless seed,
into cold currents. Like smoke, they rise,
disperse, are nothing in the darkening sky.

Above the parlor mantel now she still
is straight, her gaze sharp as the poker
on the hearth, a presence that her house, the yards,
the barns arranged themselves around; her husband
and the children in their orbits, too. Her hard
young jaw, fresh from the mountains, so definite
in this picture, now juts from my child's face
as it jutted from my father's. In that gold leaf
I see and know her more and more as I go
where she has gone. Above sad eyes, the chain
of her dark hair is wound into a crown.

www.ingramcontent.com/pod-product-compliance
Lightning Source LLC
Chambersburg PA
CBHW051948160426
43198CB00013B/2349